Jemima Foxtrot is a poet, musician, th
from Hebden Bridge, currently living i

She performs extensively and has had
BBC, the Tate Britain and Latitu
shortlisted for the Arts Foundation Spoken Word Fellowship in
2015 and her debut poetry play *Melody* was well reviewed at the
2015 Edinburgh Fringe Festival. She has performed in the Barbican
Main Hall alongside Beck, Thurston Moore and some of the UK's
leading poets including Simon Armitage and Don Paterson.

All Damn Day is Jemima's first collection of poetry.

Dear Becca,

Enjoy!

All Damn Day

Lots of love,

Jemima Foxtrot

Jemima

Burning Eye

Burning Eye Books
Never Knowingly
Mainstream

Copyright © 2016 Jemima Foxtrot

The author asserts the moral right under the Copyright, Designs and Patents Act 1988 to be identified as the author of this work.

This edition published by Burning Eye Books 2016

www.burningeye.co.uk
@burningeyebooks

Burning Eye Books
15 West Hill, Portishead, BS20 6LG

ISBN 978-1-909136-80-9

Text in italics is sung (excluding dedications and emphases). Some song fragments are composed by the poet whilst some are quoted from pre-existing traditional music.

That volatile, shape-shifting time between
the cold nights and syrupy mornings

for Mica Komarnyckyj

I told you that the transport in London is easy,
there are maps and everyone speaks your language,
at least a little bit. And you've always had
that feminine courage for asking for directions

or holding your fur coat closed at the throat,
or holding a mug of tea with both brown hands,
or holding a folder, or anything A4,
flat against your chest, with your arms crossed over it.

These are things about some women
people look at but do not appreciate.

And the good things about men:
well, the colour of their smiles is always actual,
I like them on bikes, how het up they can get,
I like the way their shoulders flex under their shirts.

The people's cheeks' London-bus-red cuts
through the vapour, their eyes are gusting out
colour through the cold. We are waylaying
drunk men and asking them to dance.

Proud to be the only two of twenty who drop
coppers in the 4am February trumpeter's sad hat,
although everyone else is enjoying it.
His fingerless gloves are retreating
up his sleeves to escape the cold.

         And we're drunk.
And confessions are dexterously revealed.

I am the fresh and wet and open eye
wedged in the bottom of all the city's coffee cups.

I am fresh and wet and the open eye
that is always looking up.

Later, back in bed with you again,
the space around each minute thickens
like an unpricked sausage,   grilling and swelling
as far as it can before its skin splits.

Living alone is like this.
Silence, like their smiles, is actual.

I saw Pete the other day.
He asked me if I'd ever watched
a couple arguing on a train.   Of course I have.

He told me, next time, to look out for the circles
in their open eyes, tune in to the loops in their discourse
and be thankful I'm out of the ring, the bottle.

I told you that the transport in London is easy;
there are maps and everyone speaks your language.

*

We have a new, locally-sourced, organic veg bag.

I remember when I was oh-so happy,
I remember the sky was shining clear and blue,
I remember how I forgot all my loneliness
'cause baby I was dancing with you.

The cauliflower sits savage in the fruit bowl on the countertop
and I am packed to the gills with the horrible claustrophobia
of a lover in my bed with a 6am start and a dear friend asleep
on the living room's pull-out couch. All this whilst burdened
by a body throbbing with insomnia. The weekend's drugs
drained out through my cold feet, my body clock rotten.

This kitchen – with mustard-coloured walls – is no place
for a girl – no woman – like me at this time on a Tuesday
night/Wednesday morning. The dryer coughs in bursts,
the cat meows -- both these things prove that I still have ears.
The fridge magnets, the map of London and the nonsense
on the chalkboard prove I still have eyes, can process things.

We have a new, locally-sourced, organic veg bag.

There is a beetroot that we need to use before Friday –
or whenever it will start to soften – glowering at me.
And earlier we played a game of thinking of things to do
with it. Asked Google. I felt horribly claustrophobic as if
companionship was all of a sudden not the answer at all,
as if the only way to keep an interesting grip on things is

discontent & trouble.

But no! People are the most important, most exciting,
we know that, don't we, mustard walls with chalkboard,
beetroot beacon, pussycat? Know too that the dredging up
of meaning from Science, religion and even the reading
of Modern Literature is sad and kind of stuffy in comparison
to a cool drink with a fabulous companion that is hot to you.

But just the other day – whilst sitting in a muted dining room
around an oval table with a cluster of lovely people –

talking about the man from British Gas coming round next day
to fix one person's boiler,

talking about a corner shop that would close soon
if custom didn't pick up,

it was whilst discussing the new Bond film
and doctor's appointments, plans for Christmas dinner,
that I was bust open with desire for a lilting domestic bliss.

I remember when I was so unhappy,
I remember when I was always feeling blue,
I remember how I clung on to my loneliness
'cause baby I was waiting, baby I was waiting.

Why is it then that now, at 3am, I am biting
            with desire for change?
Why am I already sick/scared before it's even started?

baby I was waiting for you.

*

The sun clears its throat into the sky.
We chatter crassly on as the sprouts of sleep
begin to cataract our hardened rubber eyeballs one by one.

And the boys and the girls who have found their companions
start to curl themselves around each other like shells or
balls of string. All pimpled limbs and cracked tarpaulin laughs.

The nightclub closed its doors on us and swept its floors
four hours ago now. But it's summer so our light bites
through the close-drawn curtains, tells us softly off.

Yes. The sun is coughing the streaky clouds up,
pink and red raw, as if it has shouted over shit music
all night and drunk far too many G&Ts like me.

Red sky in the morning is a shepherd's warning
but that's okay because me and my fella are praying
for rain so we can justify spending all morning in bed

sleeping and kissing and nursing our heads,
eating chocolate and watching TV.

*

The bog-eye man is the man for me,
he is blind,   he cannot see
with the bog eye,
hey-ho honey with the bog eye.
Steady on the tracks with the bog eye-oh!
He works, the bog-eye man.

The bog-eye man is the man for me,
he is blind,   he cannot see

because he is overwhelmed and controlled
by his phallus and its actions and almost matches us
in drunkenness. The rhythm of his drinking
means he doesn't blink enough and so his eyes stay glazed with
beer and his ears remain stuffed up
with the exaggerated noises of copulation.

Meanwhile

the girls have been hitting the white wine –
        hard as you like!
and endlessly applying mascara.
They're throttling all the gossip
(that's not forgotten)
from the week before
        and giggling in anticipation
of the likely night ahead.
They're busy styling their hair and shaving their legs.
They're knocking it back and jovially singing,

'The bog-eye man is the man for me,
he is blind,   he cannot see
because he's so pissed it's easy!
I can dance and drink and vomit
and the bog-eyed men still can't resist me.'

14

That is not me.   It used to be.

Now it is 3am and I'm walking home,
hiccoughing, kicking up sycamore leaves.
I am not in Manchester or Heptonstall.
I am more alone than I have ever been.

I am more at home than I have ever been.

And the shadows of the poplar trees
twitch quickly to the John Coltrane
that is pummelling my eardrums.
And I trip in time to the spasms
in my diaphragm and feel the quietness
of three o'clock, stride through the freedom
of the streets like it's Sunday morning.

Sing to myself,

Well, if you don't think you want me for
the way that I think, then I don't think
that I want you to come home.

Sing to myself in my clean bed
and watch the sun come up.
Wake up in my clean bed
still with my socks on.

Perhaps I've discovered a new kind of sanctuary
in this silvery, wintery chastity.
A chance to look, not so much at boys,
but at the wonderful world
and the women that surround me.

But the girls who came before and will come after,
who I'll no doubt be again,
are still casting their scent round every Saturday night,
never failing to find themselves some bog-eyed men.

Some men believe that they're the ones
who've got it easy, drunk and dressed down
      on a Saturday night.

These are the same men who tend to believe
all women desire to be petrified
in viscous stability,

that we're all just waiting around
until we can stay home and cook tea.

Well, everyone likes cuddles,
they allow us to forget
that the world is floating rudderless.

It's only you behind those eyes,
a dread which is mitigated slightly
when you make love,   have sex.

So we all should empathise and try to get it.

*

for Miklos Szilard

To catch our outrageous train to Birmingham I am
out in the morning before, even, the schoolchildren trickle in.

Most days I catch them tittering through the glass
at their Bunsen burners, early learners. Early men and women
             fiddling with gas taps, daydreaming of nipples.
Overbalanced from imagining a grown-up future.

Today, I'm so early I clock banker boys through the fog
on the overpass.
             I give a small, internal nod.

They are tieless, attractive,
boast strong, shaved throats, scraped teeth.

One bounces an apple on the inside of his elbow,
catches it, grinning like the moon at his lot.
This boy never takes a day off from himself.

                              *

Straight-up mornings with a full pint of tea

after John Donne
for Stephen Nashef

Oh visceral sun, go bother others
that are yet younger than us instead
as everything that matters
is sealed inside this bed.

We are whole countries caught in cotton,
hip to hip, with spittle on the pillow.
I just wish that busy old fool,
that cruel winter sun,
would piss off and leave us to it.

We are two stumps of broken teeth who,
sleeping sweetly, both are crowned
the queen and king of our cushioned domain
because nobody else is around.

We are like ammonites, coiled in bliss;
we wake with bleary lust. And, late
from punched-up alarm clocks, rush
into the city's dreary wilderness.

I swear at you, sun, through the curtains
and then give him one last kiss.

*

for Lucy Allan

The sailors touch down slap-bang
in the centre of this autumn morning.
And spread across the city as a drop
of oil in water in old washing-up.

They swear like anybody's business
but it is carefully structured swearing
and it is almost, almost, an art.

They are exceptionally dressed
like scruffy balls of otherworldliness.
Our dungareed men begin to blush.

They've cruised from Peru
and China, making money

selling bits of broken crockery,
pickled fingers, shrunken heads,
light machines, poppy seeds and lipstick.

We start to shrug them off our fantasies
like cake crumbs, but our zips and buttons
wilt atop the creaking, woodwormed deck.

The sailors have landed, my darling.
This is the best October yet.

*

It is a Tuesday morning. The house is fizzing
with late-for-work vitality as usual.

The hiss of brushing teeth pervades the landing,
hallway, kitchen.

I am tying up my laces and blindly clutching
for my keys.
            I shout for Matt to quickly fill and boil
the kettle before he leaves.
The whole house,
the world, it seems to me,
                        shouts back.

Groping at the coat rack for our brollies,
folding toast and honey round limp tongues.

We're all too regularly tempted to fester in bed,
pickled in our duvets like teenagers.

We're young travellers.
Off out onto Earth's crust each day
            like infant bears to see what we can see.

Oh, the bear went over the mountain,
the bear went over the mountain,
the bear went over the mountain
to see what he could see.
But all that he could see,
but all that he could see…

was the other side of the mountain,
the other side of the mountain,
the other side of the mountain
was all that he could see.

That's what my daddy used to sing to me
over and over
when I was a baby to keep me silent.

Now the population of this house is in its twenties,
we are hurrying into real life
like kids in damp-pyjamaed dreams.

We're drawn together at quarter past eight
to a front door that's our portal
into fun and pot luck

And as we laugh that a UKIP flyer
has been sent specifically to one of us
I am suddenly struck by the fact that we are grown-ups.

And have a place to live.   Can write an address.

I am a grown-up who wears gold shoes

I am a grown-up who dances in her bedroom

I am a grown-up whose skin is tough and I wear thick fantasies
with complicated knits.

I am a grown-up but refuse to believe it.

Since growing up the one thing I've learned
is that grown-ups aren't always that kind.

I am a child of my time.

I have never dreamt of flying and when I cry
I smoke cigarettes to regulate my breathing.

I like listening to the radio and washing plates up.

I am a grown-up who runs at pigeons
purely to prove that she can change things!
(Ditto my love of pushing the button in lifts.)

I am a grown-up who respects kids.
I give them credit for their honesty and fresh perspectives.
I am a grown-up who drinks too much
and aims, too much, to please.

I can cast a vote
and eat cold shepherd's pie for breakfast and cereal for tea.

I can entertain myself, sometimes; I can do laundry.

I can make friends, I can make love and I am lucky.

I have a ceiling to stare at from bed. I have a bed.

I can eat anything you give me now:
shellfish, liver, blue cheese.

Tomorrow we'll build a den underneath
the stairs from all our towels and blankets and sheets

and tomorrow we will stamp off our bikinis
and swim naked in the Scottish sea

because we are the grown-ups now
so it's our turn to decide what that means.

*

for Emily Cooper

I saw myself in her to-do list
that ranged from the trivial
(bathe, put clothes away, text Heather),
the type that can be crossed out, satisfyingly
ticked off, in a handful of pottering minutes,
to epic impossibilities like learn French,
read *Ulysses*, lock up Dionysus.

I saw myself in her crisis of asterisks
and hard underlinings
and in the overarching rules for life
she'd crammed down the narrowing margins,
     'Smile'   'Sort my fucking life out',
never too old to need reminding.

I saw myself in the note to self she wrote
(like I write sometimes)
that rested nestled in receipts and sweet wrappers
for when the day's behaving apathetically,

'Dear Emily, please get up and make something
of yourself. Love from some other Emily'

I saw myself in her to-do list and headscarves
and postcards and in the half-bottle of Shiraz
that had rolled beneath her bed.

I saw myself waving from the things that she said,
almost too bold and unapologetic,
in the dim Chinese restaurant on the quiet night before.

I saw myself in the shoals of discarded knickers
that littered her bedroom floor.

I saw myself in her to-do list
and I think that I liked what I saw.

*

Each day I work myself, rubbingly, away.
Each day I work myself up, up and angry.
I chafe my spirit stupid like the other commuters.
And at the end of every crummy month   I'm grateful to get paid.

But I will not get paid for noticing commuters
suspended upside down in the dark and flashing
windows of the Central line
or waving at babies on the Overground.

I will not get paid for stomping through summer thunderstorms,
the dysfunctional child of the heatwave, singing and stamping
and sodden.

I will not get paid for cleaning out the fridge.

I clock this ever-expanding city and its smiling,
vibrant people and I tell my friends,
'We really have to make the utter most of this!'
But I will not, and I will never, get paid for it.

I will not get paid for helping children write stories
or theatres raise money
or my friends make good decisions.

I will not get paid for dancing past the halal butcher's shop
that is pumping out reggae in the sunshine!

I will not get paid for listening to *Woman's Hour*
or writing plays
or making my house habitable
or going on dates.

I will not get paid for dissecting a novel
or baking a quiche
or teaching myself the piano.

But I bask in these actions nonetheless
because (my God!) they're incredible.

Oh! I feel so thunderously wonderful!
Oh, I feel so colourfully content!
Oh! I feel so thunderously wonderful!
Oh, I feel so colourfully content!

To say that money doesn't matter is a myth
perpetuated by the very rich
to whom it doesn't matter much;
they've always got enough to go to the theatre,
ride taxis, buy new shoes,
drink good wine, eat artisan meringues etc.

But I can't help but wonder if they've given up
weeping at the Good Deed Feed

scouring the reduced section

staying up late with mates trying to fix the world
(I think they've forgotten it's broken).

Walking and looking to save on bus fare

staying in and cooking pasta

drinking up and swimming in the joy of saying thank you.

I waitressed at the Association of Estate Agents' Summer Ball.
I may as well have been invisible.

I felt like saying:
I already know, you don't have to show me,
that time is moving cold and oh so slowly.

But won't forever. Wait.

I've found a little patch of grass to sit on
and wind my hard-earned happiness
between my thumb and index finger,
spindling it thinner and stronger, gathering it up,
wrapping it tight around my limbs
until it forms a pair of epic wings as tough
and complexly crafted as a spider's web
with tears, like apple pips, vibrating
on their vast and trembling surface.

Tears that sing like second hands, clicking, spitting
out each little crumb of grief,
every 'I can't do this', every layer of chip fat
on the roof of my mouth.

I try to write, there's snow outside and tannin-stained mugs
scattered like smashed glass,
half on rugs, settled next to water bottles,
under desk lamps.
Now, I don't want to be paid for poetry
or swimming in rivers and smiling
or even being nice to people.

But what I ask is inconceivable,
to exist in an oasis where it just doesn't matter.

*So when I step out into the world each morning
I see them dead-eyed and travelling,
travelling to work themselves away
ready to work themselves away.*

But I can't blame them.
We've all got bills to pay.
We've all got mouths to feed.
We've all got being involved to attend to.

*

My pet aspirin hisses at me, thwacks itself against the misty
glass, all the anger of that coked-up bouncer in one fizzing tablet.
        I feel bad.
Recently I read a Kerouac quote on a fridge magnet
in a gift shop in San Francisco; it said
'I have nothing to offer the world but my own confusion'
or something like that.
Oh wonderful searing ambivalence, pretentious youth!
        I get you, Jack.

I suffered quite the vicious thrill six years back –
tripped on a rogue cobblestone,
fell flat, impersonated a fresh-boiled lobster, obviously.
        Fell flat
with blue carrier bag in weak right hand,
blue carrier bag with raw eggs in and that was all.
Cue gasping stickiness.

It's the coquettish kettle's steam and click
that somehow makes me think of this.
It's sycophantic, my kettle.
Everybody knows that I'm a sucker for it.

        Last night
if the in-breaths of the kitchen clock were anything to go by
then we were clamped tight with excitement like oysters.

I think I lost my – no, it doesn't matter, here it is.

    Last night I caught giraffe barstools winking
as I passed, their long cow-lashes clumped with orange sleep.

My lust looped, unravelled; toilet rolls swaddling leafless trees.
My drunkenness was structured and familiar,
        my usual mug for tea.

                                *

These see-through afternoons
have just stopped listening to me

for Jimmy Eden Moon

So we stroll up there again,
that craggy scrap of footpath
to the woods round the back
of your house. Sultry rain
and bluebells. We deck its dumb
trees with our laughter. This April

dubs over the last. We've come
here each Easter for years.
Times change, the woods
stay the same. Rain, rain and
bluebells. We are muzzled

by sickly tradition so sit down
and unpack our picnic. Two
Scotch eggs, some slices of bread
and a single tepid Stella.
In this sweet smudge of wood

I love you again.
Rain and indigo bluebells.

*

for Joey Connolly

Sunday lunch, some London pub.

He says to me characteristically enthusiastically
(I sometimes wonder if that's why we're friends,
why I like him and he likes me, because of our
mutual energy for everything) that there's a blossom tree
opening at the end of his road already and brags
that that's incredible because we are only just rolling
out of January.   He has a point.

Because the black paper trees that coat the smoked London streets
are starkly silhouetted by the large and yolky sun.
It will be springtime soon enough so
we'll garrotte ourselves merrily, unintentionally,
with low-slung clichés.   I like that he doesn't brand,
doesn't stamp, the blossom with a category, apple or cherry,
          but has left it for me to decide.

I have to ask him what colour the blossom is, though.
I can't help it. He tells me it's a kind of off-white.

Now the vapid springtime imagery bounces out of its frost,
          it's broken free!
I imagine ecstatic trees frothing cotton wool, dolloped
with clotted cream, choked to the eyes with goose feathers,
trailing confetti.

          He, who is flailing in treacle-thick heartbreak but won't
let it get him down, drinks hope from the flowers.
This is useful despite the fact it's sickly. Keeps his chin
          resolutely up.

But at the stub of the previous Friday, in the thrumming hush
of my East Croydon office, the woman who sits opposite me
said she walked two laps of the cemetery at lunchtime
with her sandwich – a prawn mayonnaise baguette –
and saw (she swears!) at least five daffodils rummaging up.
Other office women scooped their hair back,
reacted in various shades of beige.

She looked at me deliberately as if she knew I understood.

I probably should've asked her to join us for lunch in the pub.

*

Brown concrete.

squirrels,

over pebbledash.
Muslim children
new-cut grass

day,' they seem

abandoned

If you go down to the woods
On Brownfield estate
is minor.
chicken

stalls, infectious

Balfron tower
jewels
It is a working spine,
breathing locals,
replenishing cells.

Lights go out.
Body shuts down.
May 26th. The blue,
blocked out

please
beginning
to yawn

A collective stretch.
their pre-prepared

Tall and crawling with

scavengers tripping hopefully

lob handfuls of

at each other. 'It is a new, safe
to holler
from their fortress (a half
slide and sandpit)

Jump! Clap! Brutalism!
today
our ice cream van's melody
And the woods are made of

shops and pigeons, market
cockney openness.

is a sceptre with living room
pushed in at night.
holding up a body of
cooking dinner,
People are being peeled off.

Spine houses ghosts.
Right now it's mid-afternoon,
negative space of sky
between the walkways,
cubism for communities
on this afternoon that's

 quite tangibly.

Soon suits will be grasping
salmon.

A collective stretch.   I am a back-door guitarist.
                               And garner smiles from all

who pass because of it.

                               I am like my dad.

I sit at the base of the stem at the back door.
Listening for the snap of communities collapsing.

*

after Sylvia Plath

It is Saturday at quarter past four pm. I've been caught
in torrential wet, pumps chucked by the door and sopping.
Stood tiptoed and bare on the end of his bed, only half
dry, eyes varnished over like glue, stupid smile.

And I rotate my acres of pale marble – dumb smile –
into the huge tense sheet of looking glass that close to covers
his back wall and I shout out, 'This is a wonderful mirror,'
and then sigh/smile, 'I could stay standing here, on the edge
of this bed, forever.' To which he laughs and pronounces me vain
like a doctor might –
　　　　'Madame, I am sorry to say that you are vain.'

I'm surprised to hear it fall off his tanned tongue,
stamp out of his foreign mouth – didn't think he'd know
that elastic word, its long sound reminiscent of hopelessness
or weather or blood. But he does. I'm surprised.
He understands it, it seems. Perhaps, I think,
　　　　he knows it himself; it's empathy.

To which I shake my hair and touch my bashed-up knees
together. Whisper, 'Of course I am, I have no
choice,' because we both know in a sackful of years
this delicious, mirrored bed I laze around in will become
my stagnant, fly-ridden lake, complete with a terrible fish.

*

I wish, I wish but it's all in vain,
I wish I was a maid again
but a maid again I never can be
'til apples grow on the orange tree.

I'm lying down with my family.   And we are here in the height
of July on a Scottish, not so hot, pebbled beach.
                        But the sun is out.

The littlest of my nieces, six and seven, are running around
in nothing but knickers, their dry cozzies rejected,
squashed at the bottom of our bags,

they're scurrying after crabs, chasing the incoming tide away,
            squealing in ripples like piglets,
getting high off the natural light,
            off the summer, off the seaside.

I wish, I wish.

They're lured back to our picnic blanket
by strawberries and apple juice and sandwiches
that have somehow got sand in them
and warm dry adult hugs
and ice cream from the van that plays
if you go down to the woods today…

Further down the beach   two older girls, about ten or
eleven, stretch out,   apprentice lionesses on beach towels,
pull giant sunglasses down on their eyes
            (so they look like flies) as they try to wisely sigh.

They behave in a way that says,
'Check me, I am doing what grown-ups do on a beach.
Check me, I might not be one but I am a teenager
and I'm doing what teenagers do,
you may think I'm just a child but you haven't got a clue.'

41

One of my little ones stops running, pot-bellied in damp pants,
and looks.

Next day, well rested and hot-chocolated and ready
for play on the beach again, it's different.
They scramble to the bottom of the bags,
chuck out the buckets and spades

and put their swimming costumes on.

Within the minute, they're laughing and splashing,
        still piglets.

I have witnessed this, in one swift moment like a photograph,
this sudden crumbling of their sweet and childish
        lack of self-consciousness like a conquered city's wall.

I have witnessed this, this milestone,
this shift in their visions that will never shift back.

I have just witnessed their rough innocence collapsing

and an origamied womanhood will grow
from their souls in its place.

I wish, I wish but it's all in vain,
I wish I was a maid again
but a maid again I never can be
'til apples grow on the orange tree.

*

Sunday looms like a derelict theme park.
I can't sleep   again.
Dearests, this is hollow laughter, tight and angry sky.

So come down with me and we will cuddle through
                    the muddled matter coiled inside our heads
and we'll sponge and spoon in the cosy cocoon
                         of my cotton-coloured
                              comedown bed.

To my best friend.
Come down with me on Saturday.
Enjoy the joys of too much weed
and shit TV to keep our sleepless demons far at bay.

Come down with me and I am sure you
will score me a seven out of ten at least.
We'll watch *One Born Every Minute*
as we clutch our wombs and weep
and the boys will have been banished from the bedroom
        (by their own volition),
they're playing *FIFA* or something.

To my lover.
Come down with me,   stay folded in the covers.
Half asleep but fully undressed,
        both ignoring your erection.
This is not about the sex at all but all about *The Simpsons*!
                    Season six in order.
And though you like sipping coffee and I like gulping tea,
we both like lying in your bed,
                    our bodies loosely touching.

To my siblings.
Come down with me, we'll laugh in our pyjamas.
          And smoke and groan, eat beans on toast.
          And reminisce about what we miss about being kids.
Trips to Devon, rain, French cricket, fishing and car-sickness,
                              then back to Devon again.
Those days when the grass was tall and the clouds were light.
Mum said the sky had been the limit
until we started getting high
              but we love each other
so we've all reached the top.

Come down alone and groan
              for real this time,
phone everyone you can think of, Mum,
pretend that you're hungover.
          Hear her mocking concern and her flicker of pride
that her daughter's a good little drinker.

Sigh down the receiver.

                Sunday looms like a derelict theme park.
                    I can't sleep   again.
I am empty, sorry sky.

Sing and hear the tones fall into the carpet.
          Cough and feel the echo.
Wish you had someone to smile at.
                Watch *The Simpsons*.
                                Sleep.

*

44

She shines right outside the swimming baths each time
I surface through the long and greasy glass swing doors;
I'm consistently hungry and red-eyed, ratty and chlorinated.

She's says that three times a week is too much,
that my youth is slipping, fish-like, away from me.
Wriggling away while my back faces the striplit, tiled sky,
        as I plough water in the fast lane.
I smile and glide right past her sometimes
as a joke.   She's like Blackpool.

When Lizzie kisses me it's nuts,
it's the dimples in crumpets humming with butter.
There is only one gemmed way to learn sex
as it should be done.   That's through this tulip,
from this Lizzie.
I am clamped around my glamorous abuser
        who has learnt to drive already.
She's got a runaround – bought for her by Mummy –
she swings me fast all over Halifax's dour roundabouts.
I perch on the passenger seat, drunk on speed
and cheeky Vimto, happy as I don't know what.
Sometimes it's almost too much for me. I cry

sometimes. She's like some half-cut, intimate Polaroid.
In her I see us both topless, tucked up
in some budget hotel bed, telly on loudly,
        the neighbours all earplugged and cursing.
I follow her into the lift. Stare at the back of her head
as if it's keeping me alive.

She lives just her and her mum, in some posh block
like a tombstone on the outskirts of town.
I have visited so often now
I know where they keep all the things that I need:
the teabags, spoons and patterned mugs, the secret biscuits.

Her mum is always working late and leaves early for work too.
So Lizzie has money to spend on me, drives me to Nando's.

When Lizzie kisses me it's nuts. The boys from school shrink,
          tongueless, in comparison.
Sometimes it's almost too much for me. I cry

sometimes. During fifth period English Lit I am clambering
into the steaming, bleached white bath at Lizzie's. I cry
sometimes.   I'm definitely giving up swimming.

*

Gloaming/best bit/sticky tar/bust

I

In the gradually darkening park
we sit and watch the boys play
football, kicking it around
like a minute chequered moon.
We grin at their beautiful lunacy.
They look at their sinewy best and,
sweating, feel omniscient, each
a throbbing god of the pitch.
One boy spits and we giggle.

II

The girls lounge, sage and amiable;
bright anchors in a world that spins
fast as our football. In the gathering
dusk they sit separate from us,
suave philosophers discussing God
knows what. So revved up,
doubting they'd talk about us,
we parade our alphabet of tricks;
all our nutmeggings and headers.

*

I am little pilgrim, little pilgrim,
         little wooden nut shell, navel-balanced.
This is my rippling pilgrimage, round zone two's
opposite notes. From Clapham to Dalston to Chalk Farm,
steady-paced pilgrim, charming.

Pistachio, green like a sculpture,
pushed through my lips by his sandpaper fingers –
bite down on his thumb pad.

Pistachios with this one in blue laptop-light
through strong and foreign cigarette smoke and wine
         from thick glass.

Ashtray and shell bowl, belly-balanced.
I have pressed each step into the pavement
to Clapham, little pilgrim, little jogging dot.

I have journeyed to see his hands' children:
sad sculpture, soft wood, mean chisel.

And, covered in sawdust, I'm lucky.
Clean under my fingernails,
         ready for our long, hot bath.

                    —

Tops of feet wet, June rain. *I am little pilgrim,*
little salty olive, winking. To Dalston,
to ash-strewn bedroom, to fucking squash risotto.
Good, young and expensive house.

I am little pilgrim and spread smiles around like butter.

Three rounds of backgammon behind us,
you're in the lead; the best of five now
and play on is the order of the day.
	More green tea, and backgammon,
		aggressive sex I'd never have expected.

Your teeth are tiny.
	I ride the last long bus home and breathe out
		finally.

—

I am little pilgrim, take the black line to a man
with twenty years on me who cooks

	home food and blows
elaborate lies like bubble-thin vomit.
Frailty's what's making you talk so much.

Little boy strode out onto the Earth's crust.
Never grew up.
	Thinks he needs to be an actor.
He needs to feel the benefit of his own hot meals.

		He needs a young mother.
		He should ignore little pilgrims
like me, trailing sooty footprints round the city,

asking for rain in Chalk Farm.

*

for Manchester

Looking up above the shop fronts
at its architecture; bricks like solidified music.
Oh, violin alleys, brass band squares

and train stations with their great threads
of strangers primed to be toppled off guard
by my grinning at them. I teach them to smile

like all those peek-a-booing babies (the babies
on the buses) and the kids in the street who sing!
Withington and Venus and the nasty mobs

of wheelie bins on my cul-de-sac's damp corners,
painted like tribesmen in flaking numbers.
I circle them past midnight to prove I'm not scared.

Turning my key into that cave-like flat,
peeling off clothes, drinking tea in the snuggest of luxury,
eating dimple-buttered crumpets with good company.

Playing records and bedroom dancing to keep warm,
catching my moon-beamed reflection in puddles,
hearing the absent ocean in the crunching leaves etc.

*

Caught on the lip of a mixing bowl.
Three eggs in a flour-well throbbing in and out of focus.
Wasp drawn to daffodil yolk, soaked
up to the neck in ketamine. Perspective shifts
seep through porous stripes, scum from a Smart Price
sponge. Fuzziness congeals into crusts around the edges.

I have been soaked up   and into the big, mean
universe I go. Drawn into egg yolks and
fruit-flavoured ciders, bubbling lava sunshine.
Soaked up into hedonism.

Caught on the lip of a mixing bowl.
Three eggs in a flour-well throbbing in and out of focus.

*

It's amazing what you can get on the internet these days.

Come   with me   baby
Your lips   taste   like anchovies
And thankfully   for you
They're my   favourite   food

And so I took your Spanish accent
            and your proud and rounded vowels
upstairs, where you were rude
about my messy, up-lit bedroom and patronised my lack.
You even managed to do that sycophantically, somehow.

You said, 'When I was poor, I slept on a mattress
I kept on the floor too. So how about I pay
            the whole of our taxi fare to get back here?'
– rolled eyes, hard smile –
            'How about I do that for you, chica?'

I said, 'Yes, great. Thank you, truly.
I've not worked for two weeks.
Just put a tenner on the dresser before you leave…
            which will be soon, right? Please?'

Then a skulking discomfort crept up my neck.

You looked round sympathetically,
emptied your pockets onto the broken table,
folded your socks into quarters
and tucked them inside your shoes.

Well, you'll never get the hot, cross love
you want from me with that attitude.

When we made it, it was boring, did you notice?

After, as soon as your belt was back on,
I wanted to flap your stiff collar
out of the crumpled corners of my deep, dim cube
of asylum, sharpish.   I don't own an iron.

You are an architect.

You may be six foot two but you stand thigh high to me
I don't like the way you move, we do it differently

But still I said –

Come   with me   baby
Your lips   taste   like anchovies
And thankfully   for you
They're my   favourite   food

Next day, despite myself, I spent some of my savings
(the ones for when the clouds make rain)
on a bed base from Gumtree.

*

He's from north-eastern Lithuania.
I congratulate his English.
If I were rich and lived here,
I would constantly call room service.

It would never work with us.
He looks after his body too much
whereas I subject mine to a lot,
I watch as it totters along.
I am young and there is no such thing
as taking too much on.
Or having too much fun.

And he is almost *too* big, *maybe,*
but gentle as an elephant.
He is stolidly building up his muscles
for carrying heavy trays and taking care
if any trouble comes our way (or so I like to think).
I grin when I run into him in the kitchen.

It would never work with us.
But I can still spend my shift
thinking of it
in the room service room
amongst the little pots of ketchup.

*

for John South

Armenia is cluttered into a restaurant on the Gloucester Road.
It's a Wednesday.   There's a wind on.
The place is charmed: stuffed with scribbling violins,
yelping, smiling clarinets. Until tonight when I pierced
into candlelight, parsley, broad beans, black-eyebrowed men,
tiny sour apples – I'd never heard clarinets sound like that.

I trace the letters of my name with my index in the humid air.
'Your name? You are English?' Yes. It's old. It's interesting.

My companion smiles.
He is sage and deaf and my age
but eighty-eight. I am twenty-four and
lick up some kind of delicious symmetry from it.

We've eaten already. They feed us.
I take my cues dancing from women
from Romania. My companion doesn't dance.

Later, in the cab back, he tells us that his father's family
were dreamers and hobbyists – his grandfather a philatelist.
His own father liked trains and measured them carefully
in their garages to craft models later.

He tells me I am drawn to men with strong jaws & strange
                                                        behaviour.
            I laugh that he lies.
He says his mother's stock were all wild men and drinkers.

So in him has always been a taste for whisky, motorcycles, Eliot,
red wine, Wales, solitude, loyalty, Music.

Next – back in his ingot living room – we can't face sleep yet, after
Armenia. He pours our nightcap.

*

There is only one way to go from here,
to slice right down the centre of the belly
with a fishhook – but no barbs – like an earring.
And remove the whole stomach, with one pull,
like a sugar cube, like a car battery or mango.

For it's the stomach that aches with the palpable,
mercury pain of heartbreak. In my dreams I ask
the clownish doctor for it, to fiddle the forms,
to re-sketch the laws, to pump all my love
for the young man down into the stomach,

then swiftly rip it out.   It's an easy procedure.

So now, in sleep at least, between the frowning
breasts and pubic bone, a scar breathes
like a watch-chain, only thinner and increasingly silver

      and I am free.

*

for Emma Williams

On Sunday night we howl
I just wanna make love to you
into mop and broom handles.

And, whirling around our cluttered
kitchen, we stamp bare feet on
discarded shards of potato peelings.

We marvel at the scandals
that have slipped in through the bricks.
We unpick each other's prettiness
and set the straight things crooked.

Now a soft knock is planted on the distant front door.
It's the two little boys who live over the road.
They're maybe six, or seven, maybe eight years old.

They present us with a rose each,
pungent and illicitly plucked
from a nicer, brighter street.

We look at each other and blush,
as pink as the flowers;
we are suddenly and stupidly touched.

*

I feel no relief when he kisses me,
only curiosity about who the next man will be.

So I'm shagging this guy from Georgia
(the country, not the state in America).
But the state that we're in when we're seeing each other
is all sharp-taloned silence, swelling questions, marijuana.

His jealousy's compelling, we eat bagels past midnight
then talk about his father before he topples into quietness,
his fists blossom; horrifying, too bright, peonies

and *I feel no relief when he kisses me,*
only curiosity about who the next man will be.

I hope the next man I wrangle with has willow vertebrae
and a kind smile.   *Why not, why not?*
A smile can go a long, long way.

I hope the next bloke I know only moves closer
          when I want him to.
This has to stop, my soul is cracking audibly.

I hope the next man I wrangle with is a habit
          that's cleaner to kick.
I hope the next bloke I know makes me feel different
when we're kissing because

I feel no relief when he kisses me,
only curiosity about who the next man will be

and I don't know why he's so hard on me,
I only shut my eyes 'cause he keeps moving closer.

*

Just so's you know I have buried your spasmodic
gaze in a pit, a shallow grave, eight inches deep
under the big symbolic sycamore tree called Nanna.
The only Nanna that I visit sometimes.

There was no ceremony to speak of but
I did do it deliberately on a Wednesday,
the day you were born.

Wednesday's child is full of woe.
Well, I've never met anybody less so.

'Who knew,' you said, when I took you up
last year, 'that the hills look royal purple from here?'
Well, it's amethyst, actually. Sorry.
I see their bruised knuckling, their dry-stone scars,
every time I come up.   Which is not much.
Honest.
There is absolutely nothing ceremonious about this.
Promise.   Promise.

I look forward to your look mulching.
You've missed the last bus home.
Sleep, bare and ignorant, under the Nanna tree.
Find yourself a fig leaf.
Grope for the too-good woodlice.

*

The conversation meanders, eroding problems as it goes.
It's somebody's birthday, winter and the windows steam up.
He discards my many arguments as if they were fish bones.
I blunder too often to the bar-cum-kitchen for more
blackish wine or strange home-labelled spirits brought back
by friends from Romania, spirits that nettle our throats,
grow us our tissue-thin layers of bravado.

Then in the wavering cube of kitchen, whilst reaching for
at least the fifth drink, I feel a thought thrust its hand
up my gullet, squeeze my wet brain in its fist, and grip it.
A revelation that there is a mug-tree on the counter with six mugs
all different shapes and patterns, bought as gifts
or out of blank necessity, all designed to drink hot drinks from.
I can touch them, spin them round my fingers by their handles.

And there's a washing machine and an old gas stove
for grilling cheese on toast or heating beans or whatever
and tea towels on a plastic rack designed specifically to hold
tea towels. There are pans hanging upside down on hooks from
the ceiling like at my mum's house and a chart telling you
which vegetables are in season. There are vegetables
in a bowl, there's a bread bin, there's a fridge with milk in.

And that this is just one flat, in one house, in one street,
in one city blah blah blah, I know you've heard it all before.
But there are millions of flats and houses all over still
with mugs and kitchen roll and wooden spoons and tampons and
condoms and teddy bears and wastepaper bins, hairbrushes, cake
tins, bubble bath, clothes pegs, pencils and pens, blankets and
pillows. Butter and bread and dishes to keep keys in.
Flats as overflowing cabinets glowing gold
          out of night's black denim.

To say this is some sudden, gut-wrenching realisation
of our tininess is reductive. It's not some
'whoa, we're all so small, man',
        despite what you're thinking, it's not that. Got that?

It's a sudden and rushing acknowledgment of the fact
that we've arrived at a place somehow where we've not just got
conflict, fundamentalism, waterborne diseases, debt, beheadings,
misogyny and slavery – but strawberries and sausages,
microscopes, takeaway menus, club-night flyers, door hinges and
padlocks. Mantelpieces, guitars, concrete
and bedsheets. A metric fucktonne of   things.

Somebody has even come up with a plastic rack you can
screw to your wall designed specifically for holding tea towels.
I like the blue and white chequered tea towels best.

The thought evaporates as quick as it came. I stutter back
into the living room's debate as if nothing ever happened.
He picks more fish bones from his teeth.

*

Oh! I'm in some saccharine haven.
How did I get here? What is it exactly
that makes this so simply angelic?
I am not in your arms in my mind
for a change but sat tight in the four walls

of my long-standing bedroom.
The same photos and postcards
Blu-Tacked up, tessellated, garland me.
A solitary Friday night for once, that's it.
No heavy men's footprints dint
my dark green carpet, nothing scuffs
my mottled rug. I am not at a party
and my window is open
at exactly the angle I like it.

Fuck! I've been waiting until now.
Stupid woman, bad attitude!
Bedroom's where it's at.
The deliberate batting away of romance
and late nights is all that it takes.
Self-sufficiency. The good life.

I am propped up on sun-faded pillows,
allowed to choose which programmes to watch.
Just me, cheap wine, my last surviving teddy.
I am in charge for once, for a welcome

change. There is a picture of the family
all together in a frame on the bookshelf;
boy, do I love it. Harks back to a happier
time with camping, with mackerel fishing.
No lover. Haven. Just limescale in the too-hot
bath and sardines in tomatoes on brown toast.
Good lonesomeness. Haven. No lover.

*

All damn day

Capital has split my dreams, a grapefruit cut in two,
the separate segments of both lives glimmering
        like a new breakfast.

A half of me wants to exist in a teepee,
        breed children who can braid hair and catch rabbits.
Drink cocoa from half Coke cans twice a year
        on their birthdays, the edges folded inwards
to protect their sleepy lips, cheap gloves to buffer their fingers,
precious marshmallows pronged on long and mossy sticks.
Wrap them in goatskin. Leave them giggling
        into drowsiness beneath the pink sky.

A half of me wants to exclude myself
                – me and some rugged, clever fella –
live in a converted, cramped van. Grow rosemary
                        and only own two dresses.
Sandals for the summer, boots for the snow.
Pick mushrooms and save them to trip from in springtime.

        Oh, rural and romantic poverty!
Lobster pots, gas lamps, home-grown tobacco,
card games, pine cones,
mussels from the shoreline filled with grit.   This is it!

It has to be.   Or something close to some of it.

I live in London.

And so yes.

And so yes, still the other half appeals to me.

If I were rich
        I'd eat asparagus and egg,
in my Egyptian-cotton-coated bed, for breakfast.   Bad. Ass.
You'd find me in my limo, got a driver called Ricardo,
wears a nice hat.   That's that.   Bad. Ass.

And if anything important breaks, there's boys around to fix it.
I'd hire the world's best campaigner
                    to make everyone a feminist.

It feels so much more comfortable to sit in these hypocrisies when
they're quilted.

And I'm in my penthouse in the middle of Paris,
            or Tokyo, or Istanbul.
The list of places that I'd like to go is endless and still growing.
But I'm rich now so don't give a shit about emissions.

I'd buy pink marigolds, plastic crystal on the finger,
fake fur around the cuffs, to pretend to my friends
            that – even though I'm rich now –
I still do my own washing-up.

Do I fuck.

My au pair's name is Clare, she's *hilarious*.
Clare's on the pots, I'm in the hot tub.

Or on my private beach in Thailand
            or asleep in the Chelsea Hotel.

Quaffing fine white wine,
scoffing oysters and the choicest cuts of beef.
There's never much grumbling going on.

Restaurants, day-spas, massages, culture, wish fulfilment.

After lunch I'll take the glider for a fly or go out to buy
a massive pile of overpriced designer tat.

That's that.   Bad. Ass.

Capital has split my dreams in two like a grapefruit.

And I want both.   And I want both.

*

for Ed Hadfield

In the summertime when the sky concertinas
            the lads cry, 'It's paradise!'
and flex in their vests. And shake their heads appreciatively
            at women. Never enough tepid Stellas
piled up high like a dunghill.
Charred, raw drumsticks punctuate the barbecue.
            It's the summertime,
            elastic days, beer gardens, fun.
We chase the sun from damp, anaemic May
until we're clinging tight with dried-out, cracking claws
            on to October
when the short nights grow like shaving foam.

But I read the other day,

whilst on an East Midlands train to Sheffield,
alongside a portly, rather thoughtful
stag party who were slurping vintage wine and burping
and discussing the economy   (one of them was snoring
heavily already and we had only really just left Leicester),

I read an essay by a man from Seattle where it rains.

And he says,

'A dripping pine is far sexier than a scorched palm tree.'

            I agree.

When the grave November rain has coloured the sky in,
            succulent, leaden, when it's tied the clouds to the mud
with chains. And my second cup of tea's grown cold and
unappealing on the chest next to the bed.

I've recently had a big invoice paid,
so I will definitely be getting us a takeaway.
There will be no venturing out of this bed today.

Darling, plant your thighs into my mattress,
let the duvet spread its roots around your legs.

But before we order we put down our books,
          folding the corners to mark the page,
yes, before we get our grub in, love,
                    then we make love again.

After the curtain's peeled back,
revealing that chewy, gristly, grey-brown rain.

Darling, plant your thighs into my mattress,
let the duvet spread its roots around your legs.

We cocoon ourselves down
          into just me and you
          and we make love again.

After scranning our Day-Glo dinner from foil,
          we lament the loss of last summer.

Sweating for what could have been forever
on that crawling bus back, just to stretch out flagrantly
          and watch the joggers run,
just to drink warm gin and tonics from bendy plastic glasses.

Enjoy the mellow buttercup tones of early evening,
mid-July.   Hear the lads cry, 'It's paradise!'
          then noisily join in with their three-a-side football.

Love, I mourn the summertime's demise
but sometimes, by September, I am craving
the terrible weather's excuse

to lie in bed with you,
        to cosily complain,
to let tea grow cold & unappealing on the chest next to the bed,

to watch the back garden's pine tree dripping.

*

You must try harder to harden your outlook and yet
still feel for others clawing through a different segment
of orange from the one that you are floating in

coolly like a retired magician. You must believe
in yourself and yet deprecate every loophole
you close with your two small hands. You must

sit quietly, watch and wait whilst the orchestra billows,
ignore it as it tells you what to do. You must try harder.
You must smile and give the people what they want.

Keep a lid on that bubbling pan. Keep your hornets'
nest mute and ticking over, just in case. Let naughtiness
rasp through the gaps between your teeth, occasionally.

You must try harder not to listen to bad advice.
'Stop caring what other people think. And please,
please, be your own woman. It is important to

find yourself.' Scrutinise your identity like overcooked
scrambled eggs. Know that the chemical change
which occurred before you turned the hob off

is irreversible. Know that you can't turn the hob off.
You must ignore chemical laws and structures.
You must try harder to remember the world

is spewing up changes, has got gut rot. You must
try harder to remember that identity's trap has half
our population snared. You must try harder to listen.

*

I've got a whistle in my soul telling me to skip town,
gospelling the parable that I'm going to have to split.
And baby, it's beginning to really look as if
I ain't never going to lose that whistle.

Still   I am sick of my own capriciousness.

Some heavy-lidded days, I honestly long for nothing more
than a bored and hoary husband and a painted fence.

For a front door just uninviting enough
                              to keep strangers away.

For prim, quiet kids who never upturn my nightly,
dark bottle on my nice cream carpets.

For a cupboard full of Tupperware
where you can invariably find all the matching lids!

But how would I breathe or write about cacti?

Other days, like today, a million images gigolo,
                    manically chat, at my peripheries.
Tangle-maned donkeys and popcorn,
sleeper trains and oranges.
A flat rock strapped to the accelerator while I sleep.
          A constant long scar of horizon.

I've watched the legs being pulled, gentle, one by one,
                              from a daddy longlegs.

It is nothing like the same grey day-to-day of England
                    in our TV static smog.

Nothing like the Domino's pizza, PG Tips
and our freshly re-elected, chinless, gutless demagogue.
And how can I sleep or write about the red sky over Yosemite
when we are sedentary

and a nationwide collective sigh has saturated our bricks?

When not giving a shit contaminates our tap water?

And yet some young women's dreams, yes!
still built tall around them keeping in their place.
Like me and my painted fence.
Like me and my weekly shop.
Like me and imagined spaghetti bolognaise every Tuesday.

But how can I roll away from here
when home means kissing under my front door's lintel
with the red paint peeling off
and never running out of places to drink in
or ways to get drunk
and the warmth of the Yorkshire accent
　　　　　　　　and raw moorland like prairies?

Let me tell you something. Sometimes I like to imagine
that in another life, before any of our times,
I was a real-life American cowboy.

I saw seventeen pretty women, each one of them on the sly.
At least I knew their names, though; I was a sometime decent guy.

　　　　　But I know I'd catch me swaggering away,
I'd grab me by my own grubby collar and I'd say,

'Hey, you little shit, you knocked my little sister up
and ran off.　　　Pathetic!
Grow yourself into the role of a bloke with a backbone.
Find a crutch you can call compassion.

I am an office assistant and I am actioning my hate on you.'

Oh, when I was a cowboy, I had that same whistle in my soul.
　　　　　I could gallop away from that hassle,
gather up my guts and get free.

*

after Jonathan Swift

I'm a woman. I'm a good one.
I'm a human and I work.   I'm a woman. I'm a good one,
so don't treat me like dirt.

Like a bored robotic shell designed to act small,
purely conservative with a small c, mouth shut,
keep schtum apart from when she's flirting.

'Don't fart, your arse is far too peachy for that.
It's better off kept just to touch and to be looked at.'

Now, I don't know about you, but
        I get too hungry to wait for my tea
and don't want to spend on a salad
                what I could on a large glass of red
so when
        I get too hungry to wait for my tea
I fold McNuggets and chips into my face
        at six in Brixton
at the back of the shop
        when I think that there's nobody watching.

It's gone viral this week, with 26,000,542 hits,
a video proving that Celia, Celia, Celia shits!

She's got ingrowing hairs from too much shaving,
and stretch marks from babies, she's got cellulite
and underneath her make-up she's got bags beneath her eyes.

She's got lungs and a colon and sinew and tissue.
Her favourite food is beans on toast,
it reminds her of her childhood.
She overcooks the chicken in the roast every Sunday.

She picks her nose like you and even, sometimes, eats it.
Yes, Celia coughs, Celia vomits,

76

Celia pisses and sneezes and shits!

Sweat drips from her pores.
But just the ones that aren't clogged up
with all that beige and sticky stuff
that she feels that she needs to be pretty.

Yes. We're burdened with this misdirected duty to obsess
           on our beauty,
           worship our skin as if it were
children,
education,
solar power.

Don't drink coffee, it stains our teeth.
Don't eat bread, don't sit down.
Gluten's the new smoking,
smoking's the new smack.

Sometimes Celia wonders if to be ladylike
is just to lie on our backs and take it.

Now, the matter in Celia's insides
is well aligned and fit for purpose.
But, unlike the diagrams, it's messy.

Blood thrusts, nerves crackle.

There are no mint-green pebbles for ovaries, no lilac fallopians,
not even an even and baby-pink triangle of womb.
Some people say that Celia was forced to grow up,
trapped into the female art of pretending,   far too soon.
Imagining she should have neat tears,   bubble breasts,
           bleached bones.

Now her legs are lame and tangled up in a net of appearance
           and reality crisscrossed.

This has got to stop.

I am not a good woman for nothing.

Because a woman isn't just for scrubbing the oven,
 popping out sprogs or dealing with your shit.
No, a woman isn't just for scrubbing the oven,
 popping out sprogs or dealing with your shit.

A woman shouldn't have to be *for* anything much.
I shouldn't have to be anything.
Celia shouldn't have had to grow up so anxious and uptight.
Always sad and scared and wondering to herself, just

what
      the *fuck*
           is ladylike?

*

after Tracey Emin

Bed as psyche.   Bed as mother.   Bed as everything.

Messy. Stained.   Paraphernalia, all rubbish
pretty much, tell stories like smells do.
                    The way you make my sheets smell.

Sheets as neuroses so their coming unstuck
from the mattress is a good thing.

I am the goddess of the kingdom of my filth.

You are so lucky to see my slippers.
You would be lucky to touch my feet.

Pregnancy test as peephole, negative test as gaping blue sky

Condom as contradiction. Nail scissors used to trim pubes
as redemption.
Tidiness as long-held promise.

Room as ever-expanding universe.

Loose change as photographs,   Polaroids as currency.
I have let you look inside my bedroom. Now I'm a celebrity.

Barbecue sauce from McDonald's as distant, drunken memory.
Vodka as clothing,   tealight as family.

*

79

The fashionable aspect of place in poetry is not a red herring.
Still, it's not nice to believe we are tied to our childhood home.

We are Yorkshire. We are hills and sheep and steel
and oh my God geographical hold is pressing my spineless self
into this new, unbending tarmac. I often dream of superglue,
a jungle of smashed-up mugs and shattered soup bowls.
I always ask my mummy what to do, she never knows.
I dream of rinsing several layers of oil off.
I hope that my dreams mean nothing.

Geographical hold is dark beer that looks like piss,
it is gleaming vistas of moorland jaundiced with gorse,
it's that exact shade of green that screeches 'home!'
when you least expect it.   North Wales
        has that same shade too.
It is glottal-stopping jobsworths on grimy, clattering trains.
It's the fact my accent broadens with every year I spend away.

We are oppressive rain   and laughter in its face.
We are pancake mix risen into puddings
and deep, steep-sided valleys, we are Boxing Day walks.
We are the bloody-minded surety
our kids will be from Yorkshire, somehow, just like us.

We are the Trades Club, its barn-owl roof juddering
from bass. We are hazy bluebell woods.
We are the twenty or more Huddersfield drug dealers
all called Mud. Oh my God, geographical hold

is a million invisible strings fastened tight to the top
of our too-human heads. I often dream of superglue.

It is the misplaced but weighty guilt
of fleeing to the stark and thrilling city.

We are decidedly London for now.
We are skint and have nowhere to settle.

*

for Olivia and Sami

Whilst I am waiting for the 37 home from Brixton or snug in a booth all warm brown at the Gowlett or in the queue to buy eggs from the big Asda or collecting goldfish train tickets from the mean machines at King's Cross again, folk are crafting plans to see each other next time. Arrangements are made – 'sooner this time, eh?' – arms loop around eclectic backs in hugs goodbye, every setting everywhere is brimming with handshakes and back pats.

Let me dig into these myriad scenes for a second.

A mother is saying, 'Don't forget to call Janey tomorrow,' like a moralising sparrow to her antsy tattooed daughter who replies that she won't and one woman is telling another to remember her thing on the twenty-third, to put it in her diary, that she'll be trying out a new recipe, something vegetarian now that her girls have turned, smile/sigh but 'it'll be so good to have everyone together'. And I decide, while I'm waiting to pay for my eggs in the dawdling queue, that it will. I wish briefly but intensely that I could be there too.

A man is rambling with a pint and a beard like a poltergeist about his father's long service in the Second World War and a couple of blokes are dismembering some absent woman's 'crazy' behaviour and motives. On the table on the way to the toilets, a family with grown-up children is playing snap with giant playing cards the size of encyclopaedias that the dad got for Christmas in his office Secret Santa. They look funny. They're pulling a crowd in around them like a playground fight. One dressed-up woman lends her lipstick in the loo to another dressed-up woman. Emergency toilet roll is passed under cubicle walls. Couples kiss. Babies are handed round and roundly cooed at. Almost everyone eats pizza.
Once I sang

an improvised song about when the 37 would show up while I was waiting in Brixton for the 37 to show up, some women joined in and we were suddenly chanting, even harmonising together and the bus came like a saviour, I like to think because of our fabric of song, and we poured on to it like sugar. One evening a barman gave me more than a fiver in change when I paid him with a fiver and it made my fucking week. I almost started fitting the first time I bumped into someone I knew on the street in London. It was too much.

Some youngish, well-dressed, mixed-sex group grieve the dismantling of the NHS, house prices, make vague cases for other cities that should star in their stubbly futures. A man waiting at the station squeals, his suitcase-laden sister bashes bull-like into his arms. A walking-sticked woman strokes a tabby cat. A woman running for a bus hurries down her mobile that she'll call her mother back. A shopkeeper hands a snotty toddler a lolly. And this continues

all damn day, all damn fullocky, wonderful day.

All this blethering, all this affection, all the speculation, all this future, all these nuisances, all this outrage and wonderment, fear and heavy-bottomed joy is replicated in cities and villages. Versions of this exist in every second all over the folded-out surface of our world.

I'm too grateful for it – it's too good.

*

Notes

Page 12: *The bog-eye man is the man for me,/he is blind, he cannot see* … is adapted from the traditional English folk song 'Hog-Eye Man'.

Pages 20 and 21: *The bear went over the mountain* … is from the traditional English song 'The Bear Went Over the Mountain'.

Pages 38 and 40: *I wish, I wish but it's all in vain,/I wish I was a maid again* … is from the traditional English folk song 'I Wish'.

Page 72: *A dripping pine is far sexier than a scorched palm tree* is adapted from an essay by Tom Robbins in *Wild Ducks Flying Backward*, New York: Bantam, 2005.

Acknowledgments

Thanks to Luke Wright for seeing value in what I do, for trusting me and kicking me into this world. Huge thanks to Clive Birnie for supporting and publishing my first ever book! Big thanks to the Arts Foundation and the judging panel for the 2015 Spoken Word Fellowship; my shortlisting brought me recognition, confidence and some much-needed financial freedom to focus on my work. Thanks to Mike Hodson for designing the happy book cover for me. Huge thanks to the Clapham Omnibus for all that free space and support. Massive thanks to Patrick Lawrence for wading through the legal quagmire of using song lyrics in poetry books.

Thanks to the New Student Writing Society of the University of Manchester (2008–2011), with especial thanks to Lucy Allan, James Horrocks and Stephen Nashef, and particular thanks to Joey Connolly; without our chats that try to navigate the world and poetry none of this could've happened. Massive thanks to the ever-best and kindest Ed.

Eternal thanks to my incredible family – especially Mum and Dad – without whom I would not be the person I am and could not have written this book.

And finally, cheers to all of my friends and lovers past, present and future – thanks for helping me make my days.

Lightning Source UK Ltd.
Milton Keynes UK
UKHW010439140919
349739UK00003B/281/P

9 781909 136809